50 Games for Going Green

Physical Activities That Teach Healthy Environmental Concepts

Carol Scaini

Carolyn Evans

Human Kinetics

Library of Congress Cataloging-in-Publication Data

Scaini, Carol.
  50 games for going green : physical activities that teach healthy environmental concepts / Carol Scaini and Carolyn Evans.
    p. cm.
  ISBN-13: 978-1-4504-1990-1 (soft cover)
  ISBN-10: 1-4504-1990-9 (soft cover)
  1. Physical fitness for children. 2. Environmentalism. I. Evans, Carolyn, 1957- II. Title.
  GV443.S228 2012
  613.7'042--dc23

                                          2011052794

ISBN-10: 1-4504-1990-9 (print)
ISBN-13: 978-1-4504-1990-1 (print)

The web addresses cited in this text were current as of February 2012, unless otherwise noted.

Acquisitions Editor: Scott Wikgren; **Developmental Editor:** Jacqueline Eaton Blakley; **Assistant Editor:** Anne Rumery; **Copyeditor:** Annette Pierce; **Permissions Manager:** Dalene Reeder; **Graphic Designer:** Joe Buck; **Graphic Artist:** Denise Lowry; **Cover Designer:** Keith Blomberg; **Photographer (cover):** © Human Kinetics; **Art Manager:** Kelly Hendren; **Associate Art Manager:** Alan L. Wilborn; **Illustrations:** © Human Kinetics; **Printer:** McNaughton & Gunn

Printed in the United States of America   10 9 8 7 6 5 4 3 2 1

The paper in this book is Forest Stewardship Council™ certified.

FSC
www.fsc.org
MIX
Paper from
responsible sources
FSC® C011935

Human Kinetics
Website: www.HumanKinetics.com

United States: Human Kinetics, P.O. Box 5076
Champaign, IL 61825-5076
800-747-4457
e-mail: humank@hkusa.com

Canada: Human Kinetics, 475 Devonshire Road Unit 100, Windsor, ON N8Y 2L5
800-465-7301 (in Canada only)
e-mail: info@hkcanada.com

Europe: Human Kinetics, 107 Bradford Road, Stanningley
Leeds LS28 6AT, United Kingdom
+44 (0) 113 255 5665
e-mail: hk@hkeurope.com

Australia: Human Kinetics, 57A Price Avenue, Lower Mitcham, South Australia 5062
08 8372 0999
e-mail: info@hkaustralia.com

New Zealand: Human Kinetics, P.O. Box 80, Torrens Park, South Australia 5062
0800 222 062
e-mail: info@hknewzealand.com

E5588

To my mom and dad. Thank you for instilling in me a passion for health and physical education and for your love and support. xoxo

To my nieces and nephews. Life is short: find your passion, dream often, inspire others, make a difference, be active, leave the world a better place, and eat ice cream! xo

Remembering my professor, colleague, mentor, and friend, Dr. Andy Anderson.

—Carol Scaini

For my family and in memory of my mom.

—Carolyn Evans

CONTENTS

Game Finder   vi

Acknowledgments   ix

Introduction   xi

1 Warm-Up Activities 1

2 Relays 19

3 Circuit and Station Activities 35

4 Literacy and Drama Activities 51

5 Fitness Activities 63

6 Cooperative Activities 87

50 Ways to Pitch in and Do Your Part   105

Recommended Resources   109

About the Authors   111

GAME FINDER

Game	Game type	Activity level	Play area	Page
3-R Challenge	Warm-up	Medium, high	Classroom, gym, outdoors	8
Back to Nature	Fitness	Medium, high	Classroom, gym, outdoors	68
Bin Ball Recycling	Cooperative	Low, medium	Classroom	88
Can You . . . ?	Literacy and drama	Medium, high	Gym, outdoors	59
Compost Bug Tag	Warm-up	Medium, high	Gym, outdoors	14
Do Your Part	Literacy and drama	Medium, high	Classroom, gym, outdoors	62
Don't Be a Litter Bug!	Fitness	Medium, high	Gym, outdoors	74
Eco Olympics	Circuits and stations	Medium, high	Gym, outdoors	41
Environment Tag	Warm-up	High	Gym, outdoors	2
Environmental Crosswords	Literacy and drama	Medium	Gym	52
Every Little Bit Counts	Relays	Medium, high	Gym, outdoors	24
Extinction	Warm-up	Low	Classroom, gym, outdoors	18
Flower Power (Rock, Paper, Scissors)	Warm-up	Medium, high	Classroom, gym, outdoors	6
Get Active! Go Green!	Warm-up	Low, medium	Classroom, gym, outdoors	11
Get Outside and Play: Fall Fitness	Fitness	Medium, high	Gym, outdoors	84
Get Outside and Play: Spring Fitness	Fitness	Medium, high	Gym, outdoors	80
Get Outside and Play: Summer Fitness	Fitness	Medium, high	Gym, outdoors	82
Get Outside and Play: Winter Fitness	Fitness	Medium, high	Gym, outdoors	78
Green Power	Literacy and drama	Medium	Gym, outdoors	56
Green-Team Catch	Cooperative	Medium, high	Gym, outdoors	96
Green-Thumb Gardeners Tag	Warm-up	Medium, high	Gym, outdoors	16
Healthy-Environment Charades	Literacy and drama	Medium	Gym	54
Imagine . . .	Literacy and drama	Low	Gym, outdoors	58
Keep on Recyclin'	Cooperative	Medium	Gym, outdoors	100

Game	Game type	Activity level	Play area	Page
Knock out Pollution	Cooperative	Low, medium	Gym, outdoors	92
Litter Not!	Cooperative	High	Gym, outdoors	90
Living Things	Warm-up	Medium, high	Classroom, gym, outdoors	12
Move It: Reduce, Reuse, Recycle	Cooperative	Medium, high	Gym, outdoors	94
On the Move With Endangered Animals	Literacy and drama	Medium, high	Gym, outdoors	60
Paper-Ball Fitness	Fitness	Medium, high	Classroom, gym, outdoors	67
Pitch In	Relays	Medium	Gym, outdoors	26
Plant a Tree With TLC	Relays	Medium, high	Gym, outdoors	20
Plight of the Polar Bear	Circuits and stations	Medium, high	Gym	47
Pollution Tag	Warm-up	High	Gym, outdoors	4
Put Your Best Foot Forward	Literacy and drama	Low	Gym, Outdoors	57
Ready, Set, Compost	Cooperative	High	Gym, outdoors	98
Recycling-Bin Basketball	Cooperative	Medium, high	Gym, outdoors	102
Reduce, Reuse, Recycle Challenge	Fitness	Medium, high	Gym, outdoors	76
Reducing Litter	Relays	Medium, high	Gym, outdoors	22
Reeeuse! Reeecycle!	Fitness	Medium	Gym, outdoors	70
School Yard Fitness	Circuits and stations	High	Outdoors	40
Sock It to Ya!	Circuits and stations	Medium	Gym, outdoors	38
Step up to Recycling	Relays	Low, medium	Gym, outdoors	30
Take a Pass on Pollution	Fitness	Medium, high	Classroom, gym, outdoors	72
Take Care of the Earth	Relays	Low, medium	Gym, outdoors	28
Three Cheers for Planet Earth	Relays	Medium, high	Gym, outdoors	32
Trash Ball Fitness	Circuits and stations	High	Gym, outdoors	36
Trees! Trees! Trees!	Warm-up	Medium, high	Classroom, gym, outdoors	10
Whole World in Your Hands	Fitness	Medium	Gym	64
Working out for the Environment	Circuits and stations	Medium, high	Gym	44

ACKNOWLEDGMENTS

Special thanks to our students who played our games and provided us with creative ideas for new games and activities.

Thank you to the team at Human Kinetics for their support.

Thank you, Scott Wikgren, for your direction, support, and enthusiasm for all things green!

Thank you, Jackie Blakley—your support and expertise were greatly appreciated and made fine tuning the book a real pleasure.

INTRODUCTION

We often take our environment for granted. The air we breathe, the water we drink, the land we walk on, the food we eat, the trees and plants and animals, these are all essential for us to live healthy lives. But they are increasingly threatened by destructive choices we make— wasting resources, littering, failing to take into account the collective effects of our carelessness.

50 Games for Going Green is a resource for teachers and youth leaders to educate students about the importance of caring for the environment through the use of fun physical activities. The book is filled with simple games and activities that we hope will not only engage our students in physical activity, but also inspire them to become environmental stewards who appreciate and take care of the earth.

The book focuses on educating students about the importance of the three Rs—reducing, reusing, and recycling. As teachers, we have found that emphasizing the value of reducing, reusing, and recycling through fun and innovative games has helped to generate excitement in our students to help them get active and go green.

Lessons are fast, fun, ecofriendly, and easily modified to suit a variety of ages, abilities, and skill levels. These activities can be played in a variety of settings and require little or no equipment; in fact, many allow you to use everyday recyclable items that are easily found at home or school. One person's trash is another person's treasure, so why not make cards from recycled paper, balls from socks, and bowling pins from plastic bottles? When students try to find new uses for recyclable items, they are inspired to be creative thinkers, active players, and environmental protectors. The games and activities in this book also provide a wonderful opportunity for students to demonstrate cooperation, fair play, and respect, not only for each other, but also for our world.

Although this book is written primarily for physical educators, anyone involved in leading physical activities (e.g., classroom teachers, Scout and Girl Guide leaders, recreational leaders, outdoor education instructors) will also find these games to be useful.

HOW THE BOOK IS ORGANIZED

The book is divided into six chapters that cover the following topics:

- **Warm-up activities** get students moving and learning about the environment.
- **Relays** are a fast and fun way for students to work in teams to accomplish a task related to an environmental theme.
- **Circuits and stations** are easy to follow and aim to keep students moving and improve overall fitness.
- **Literacy and drama activities** engage the mind and body by allowing students to think while being active.
- **Fitness activities** allow students to exercise their entire body in various physical challenges.
- **Cooperative activities** are positive, motivating, and fun. They promote teamwork, creative thinking, and problem solving.

Each chapter contains a variety of games and activities that can be used in the gym, classrooms, and outdoors. They also include activity and game instructions along with a diagram to illustrate how to play.

An easy-to-follow format provides detailed instructions for introducing games and activities.

SAFETY

It is important to provide an environment that encourages and enables students to engage in safe and enjoyable physical activity. Before conducting the activities in this book, consider the following tips for ensuring a safe environment:

- Check surrounding area and eliminate potential hazards before use.
- Encourage students to report problems to the teacher or leader.
- Check all equipment before use to ensure all equipment is safe and in good working order.
- Ensure recyclable materials are clean.
- Ensure students use equipment for its intended purpose.
- Ensure students wear suitable footwear and clothing.
- Be aware of medical conditions of participating students.
- Establish rules and routines.

PITCH IN

Eco Thought

Recycling can be easy when we all pitch in
how you can get recycling bins at your s
program. Recycling is good for all of us.

Eco Thought
Provides basic environmental information
for your students to think about, discuss,
and take action on

Equipment

- A variety of recyclable materials (e.g., w
  aluminum cans, plastic containers) or a
  beanbags, skipping ropes, balls, scoops)
  student
- 2 recycling bins
- Stopwatch or gym clock

Equipment
Describes the equipment required for the game
or activity (We have added music to activities
where we feel it will help motivate the students.
Music is always optional in our activities.)

Setup

- Divide players into two teams, forming two lines.
- Place an empty recycling bin at the end of each line and half of the
  recycling items at the beginning of each line.

How to Play

1. On the go signal, both team   their
   line.

Setup
Provides information to help prepare the
game or activity

2. The first player passes the i   econd
   o passes it through his or her legs to the third player, who
   ver his or her head, and so on.

How to Play
Provides simple instructions for
game play

eam to safely recycle all of its materials can cheer, "We
pitched in!"

Note

Ensure recyclable items are safe and clean.

Note
Offers safety considerations and special
reminders for game play
Encourages students to take a leadership
role and challenges them to create their
own games

Variations

- Change the method of passing the re
  only, knees only, feet only, sideways).
- M   he last player in line can pitch it
  in   nt way of pitching it each time
  (e   erhand, set shot, with both feet,
  ba

Variations
Presents new ways to play the game or
activity and new challenges

- Ensure everyone has an equal chance to play.
- Provide activities that are age appropriate.
- Encourage respect and fair play.

It is our hope that teachers will recognize the need to educate their students about the important role they play in protecting our earth. Learning through activity will engage students to take this knowledge and apply the ideas to their own lives. This can be as simple as reconnecting with the great outdoors or making a commitment to reduce, reuse, and recycle. Or it can be as complex as exploring ways to reduce their carbon footprint and take action on global warming and climate change. Take the games in this book and make them your own. Have fun playing them, building on them, changing them, and creating new ones. Inspire your students to come up with their own creative ideas and together have fun going green.

What happens in one part of the world can have a great impact on another part of the world. We must all work to protect our beautiful earth by taking strong steps to respect it, enjoy it, and take care of it. It all starts with you!

CHAPTER

WARM-UP ACTIVITIES

Take care of the earth and she will take care of you.
—Author unknown

Warm-up games are simple activities that get students moving. They serve as *instant activities* to prepare students for skill development and are a great way to help spark excitement about participating in subsequent games.

ENVIRONMENT TAG

Eco Thought

Millions of recyclables such as fine paper, plastic water bottles, and aluminum cans are thrown into the garbage every day instead of being placed in recycling bins. By making an effort to recycle more, we create far less pollution and reduce the amount of unnecessary waste in landfills. Think of all of the new materials that could be made if we just recycled more.

Equipment

- Music
- 4 beanbags of the following colors:
  - Green: reduce
  - Red: reuse
  - Blue: recycle
  - Brown: compost
- Environmental fitness signs for each corner of the playing areas:
  - Reduce: the twist (while moving the body up and down)
  - Reuse: jumping jacks
  - Recycle: bicycle pumps
  - Compost: push-ups

Setup

- Divide the playing area into four fitness areas representing reduce, reuse, recycle, and compost.
- Select four students to be the environmental taggers, one for each area: reduce, reuse, recycle, compost.

How to Play

1. Students move freely around the area trying to avoid being tagged by one of the four environmental taggers.
2. Once a student is tagged, he or she must go to the fitness area represented by that tagger and perform the fitness task. For example, if the reduce tagger tags a student, he or she must go to the reduce area and do the twist up and down while jumping.
3. Once a tagged student completes the fitness task, he or she may return to the game.

Notes

- Change the four environmental taggers often throughout the game.
- Vary the fitness tasks.

POLLUTION TAG

Eco Thought

Pollution affects the health of people, animals, and the planet. We can all do our part to keep pollution at bay by making a better effort to reduce, reuse, and recycle.

Equipment

Music

Setup

- Divide students into groups of four.
- Three students form a triangle by holding hands. These three students represent reduce, reuse, and recycle. Student four represents pollution.

How to Play

1. Pollution is the tagger on the outside of the triangle.
2. Pollution chooses to tag either reduce, reuse, or recycle.
3. The reduce, reuse, and recycle students in the triangle try to protect each other by moving the group around to the left or to the right to prevent pollution from tagging the designated student. Reduce, reuse, and recycle students must remain attached, and pollution is not allowed to go through the triangle to tag.

Notes

- Students need to be in the ready position so that they are able to move and change direction quickly:
  - Feet shoulder-width apart
  - Knees slightly bent

- One foot slightly ahead of the other
- Head up, chest out with hands out in front
- Change the pollution tagger frequently to ensure that everyone has a chance to be the tagger.

Adapted, by permission, from P. Doyle, 2001, Triangle tag. In *Tag, tag and more tag* (Ontario, Canada: Canadian Intramural Recreation Association of Ontario), 26.

FLOWER POWER

Eco Thought

Life for a flower begins as a tiny seed. When nurtured with sunlight, clean water, air, and rich soil, the tiny seed grows into a healthy, beautiful flower. Help nurture nature by planting a seed for a greener future.

Equipment

Music

Setup

Before playing, review the actions of the rock, paper, scissors game:

- Reduce (rock) beats recycle (scissors).
- Reuse (paper) beats reduce (rock).
- Recycle (scissors) beats reuse (paper).

How to Play

1. Students move around the playing area in a crouched position representing seeds.
2. When they encounter another seed, they play rock, paper, scissors (RPS).
3. Play begins when partners say ready and then at the same time shake their fists while saying, "reduce, reuse, recycle" (instead of "one, two, three"), before showing a hand signal:
   - Reduce (rock): fist
   - Reuse (paper): flat hand
   - Recycle (scissors): two fingers
4. The loser remains a seed and looks for another seed to play RPS, while the winner becomes a stem who now can move around the space lunging with hands clasped and arms straight above the head, looking for another stem.
5. When the winner finds another stem, these two play RPS.
6. The winner becomes a flower who walks around with arms swaying back and forth above the head like a blossoming flower. The loser should find another stem to play RPS.
7. When two flowers play, the winner becomes a bouquet that jogs around giving high fives to other bouquets.
8. Once a student becomes a bouquet, he or she no longer has to play RPS.

Note

Seeds can only play seeds, stems can only play stems, and flowers can only play flowers.

Variation

When students lose, they begin the life cycle again and become a seed.

Adapted, by permission, from CIRA, 2003, Evolution. In *Why paper & scissors rock!!* (Ontario, Canada: Canadian Intramural Recreation Association of Ontario), 25, 26.

3-R CHALLENGE

Eco Thought

How can you and your family have less of an impact on the environment?

- Buy less to reduce waste.
- To get the most out of what you purchase, reuse it.
- To create less pollution, recycle.

Equipment

Poster board or a whiteboard

Setup

- Write the rock, paper, scissor actions on poster board or a whiteboard for students' reference.
- Before playing, review the rock, paper, scissors actions:
  - Reduce (rock) beats recycle (scissors).
  - Reuse (paper) beats reduce (rock).
  - Recycle (scissors) beats reuse (paper).
- Divide the class into two groups.
- Students stand in straight lines, each facing a partner across the middle of the playing area.

How to Play

1. Students play one game of 3-R Challenge (rock, paper, scissors).
2. Play begins when partners say ready and then at the same time shake their fists while saying, "reduce, reuse, recycle" (instead of "one, two, three"), before showing a hand signal.
   - Reduce: fist
   - Reuse: flat hand
   - Recycle: scissors
3. The students who lose remain in their spots.
4. The students who win run to the end of the gym, touch the wall, and come back to find a new partner to challenge.

Variations

- Students who win may perform a physical activity on the spot, while their opponents run to the wall.
- The winning student suggests a physical activity for his or her opponent to perform (e.g., 10 jumping jacks).

Adapted, by permission, from CIRA, 2003, Evolution. In *Why paper & scissors rock!!* (Ontario, Canada: Canadian Intramural Recreation Association of Ontario), 28.

TREES! TREES! TREES!

Eco Thought

Have you hugged a tree today? Trees are our friends. They help to clean the air we breathe, keep us cool, and give us food to eat. Trees also provide a home and shelter for wildlife. Find ways to take care of the trees in your community.

Equipment

- Chart paper
- Markers

Setup

Chart the following commands and distribute or post them:

Oak tree—Put your hand on your heart for national pride (American).
Maple tree—Put your hand on your heart for national pride (Canadian).
Green leaf—Crouch to the floor and spring into the air.
Pine needle—Stand straight with arms over your head.
Seed—Curl up tightly, then uncurl one *leaf* at a time and stretch.
Tree hugger—Hug yourself, or find a friend for a three-second hug.
Acorn—Curl into a ball and rock and roll yourself on the spot.
Chestnut—Reach arms out and in to tap your head.
Poison ivy—Scratch all over.
Apple tree—Reach up and pretend to pick an apple.
Mulch—Lie flat on the floor.
Make like a tree and leaf—Run to a designated place.

How to Play

1. Call out the commands. Students perform the actions continuously until the next command is called.
2. Challenge students to come up with new commands.

Note

Students may research to find the tree that represents their country as a symbol of strength and national pride. For example, the maple tree is known as Canada's tree, and the United States is known for its oak trees.

Adapted, by permission, from C. Scaini, 2007, *Fun classroom fitness routines ages 10-14,* DVD (Champaign, IL: Human Kinetics).

Eco Thought

Getting outside to play is a great way to get active and show your appreciation for nature. Enjoy what Mother Nature has to offer and take action to protect it. What can you do to show that you care about nature?

Equipment

- Chart paper
- Markers

Setup

- Divide the class into two groups.
- Select one leader for each game: Eco Emily or Green Griffin.
- Chart the following commands and distribute or post them:

Go for a hike—March on the spot.

Clean up litter—Bend and reach.

Rake the leaves—Perform a raking action.

Dig the earth to plant a tree—Make a shoveling action.

Switch off the lights—Reach and flick your wrist.

Go for a run—Run around the perimeter of the playing area.

Pull out the weeds—Bend and pretend to pull weeds from the ground.

Paddle a canoe—Show a paddling action.

How to Play

1. Each leader begins by announcing, "Eco Emily says . . . " or "Green Griffin says . . . " and selects an activity from the list on the chart.
2. If Eco Emily or Green Griffin catches someone doing the action without the prompt "Eco Emily says" or "Green Griffin says," the student moves to the other side of the playing area to join the other game.

Variations

- Challenge students to create new environmental actions.
- Invite your whole school to participate in a giant game in the school yard.
- Each class starts its own Eco Emily Says or Green Griffin Says game.
- If Eco Emily or Green Griffin catches someone doing the action without the prompt, the student caught moves to another class's game.

Eco Thought

Mother Earth and most living things need healthy soil, clean water, clean air, and sunshine not only to survive, but also to thrive. When you are enjoying nature, remember to leave it the way you found it. Take your garbage or recyclables home and do your part to keep the planet clean.

Equipment

- Colored cards
- Chart paper
- Markers
- Music

Setup

- Create a chart listing the basic needs of all living things along with the movement and color associated with each:
  - Earth: mountain climbing (green card)
  - Water: front crawl swimming action (blue card)
  - Air: running around the playing area, pumping arms (white card)
  - Sun: star jumps (yellow card)
- Create a set of colored cards that represent the basic needs of all living things.
- Create an equal number of cards in each color.
- Provide one colored card to each student.

How to Play

1. Students move around the playing area exchanging the cards with one other.
2. When the music stops, all movement stops and students perform the fitness activity according to the color of the card they are holding.
3. Continue playing.

Note

Invite students to create their own fitness activities.

Adapted, by permission, from Peel District School Board, 2006, *Hooked on DPA-Daily physical activity* (Mississauga, ON: Peel District School Board).

COMPOST BUG TAG

Eco Thought

Composting is nature's way of recycling. Healthy compost requires soil, water, air, dead leaves, plants, and peelings. Start composting today, and it won't be long before you have your own nutrient-rich garden soil for plants to grow in.

Equipment

- 4 beanbags of different colors
- Music

Setup

- Select four students to be taggers representing compost ingredients:
  - Peels and greens: green beanbag
  - Leaves and soil: brown beanbag
  - Water: blue beanbag
  - Air: yellow beanbag
- All other students represent sow bugs and millipedes.

How to Play

1. Compost taggers chase the sow bugs and millipedes in the playing area trying to tag them.
2. Tagged bugs lie on their backs with their arms and legs in the air.
3. Tagged bugs may only reenter the game when four free sow bugs or millipedes hold the tagged bug's outstretched hands and feet.
4. Once the four students are attached, together they call out "One, two, three, compost" and begin to play again.

Notes

- Change bugs after a few minutes.
- Before playing, ask students what ingredients go into producing healthy compost.

GREEN-THUMB GARDENERS TAG

Eco Thought

Gardens make our world a beautiful place. Creating a garden is a healthy form of exercise and is a simple way to connect and care for the world we live in. Beautify your yard with flowers or grow great things to eat. Get going! Get growing!

Equipment

- 1 or 2 green beanbags
- 2 or 3 brown beanbags

Setup

- Select two or three taggers to be the weeds and give them the brown beanbags.
- Select one or two students to be the green-thumb gardeners and give them the green beanbags.
- All other students represent the flowers and vegetables in the garden.

How to Play

1. Students move freely around the playing area while the weeds attempt to tag them by tapping them gently with the beanbags.
2. Tagged students are frozen in a crouched position with their thumbs up.
3. Students may be rescued only by the green-thumb gardeners, who tap the frozen students on their roots (toes) with the green beanbags.
4. Once free, the student *grows* back into the game by *sprouting* (jumping up).

Notes

- Change the weeds and gardeners often throughout the game.
- Depending on your class size, additional equipment and taggers may be introduced.

Eco Thought

Forests are home to many kinds of wildlife. We can help to keep animals off the endangered species list or keep them from becoming extinct by protecting their natural habitat. Recycling paper helps to keep trees from being cut down, allowing our animal friends to keep their homes.

Equipment

- Chairs
- Music

Setup

Set up chairs in a circle with their backs facing each other. Use one chair less than the number of students playing.

How to Play

1. Players stand in a circle around the chairs before the music begins.
2. Once the music starts, players move in a line around the chairs.
3. When the music stops, all players immediately sit in a chair.
4. The player without a chair is *extinct* because his or her natural habitat has disappeared.
5. Play again, removing one chair from the circle each round.

Variations

- No chairs? Students sit on the floor, and the last person to sit becomes extinct.
- Use poly spots instead of chairs.

CHAPTER

RELAYS

We do not inherit the earth from our ancestors, we borrow it from our children.

—Native American proverb

Relays are a fast and fun way to get students physically active while achieving a goal. They provide an opportunity for students to actively participate and to demonstrate cooperative skills, teamwork, and fair play. Win or lose, we are all cheering each other on to help protect the environment.

PLANT A TREE WITH TLC

Eco Thought

For a tree to grow and flourish, it needs clean air, clean water, healthy soil, sunlight, and a little TLC. TLC means that we show tender loving care not only for our tree but also for our environment and all living things.

Equipment

1 pylon per team

Setup

- Divide the players into teams of five. Each team member represents one of the following: clean air, clean water, healthy soil, sunlight, and a little TLC. If the teams are uneven, they should pretend to pick up teammates so that each team makes the same number of runs.
- Place one pylon 30 to 60 feet (10-20 m) away from each team on the opposite side of the playing area.
- Line up players one behind the other, forming one line for each team.

How to Play

1. The first player (clean air) runs to the pylon, around it, and then back to the team to pick up the second player (clean water) by grabbing hands. Players must remain attached by holding hands.
2. Together they run to the pylon, around it, and then back to the team to pick up the third player (healthy soil) by holding hands.
3. Continue until everyone has been picked up and completes the relay.
4. The first team to successfully plant a tree will have all players standing together with their arms outstretched over their heads, resembling a forest of trees.

Variations

- Vary the distance according to the age and grade level.
- Change the method of locomotion.

Eco Thought

When we recycle, we help to keep waste from ending up in landfills. Landfills are huge holes in the ground filled with garbage. Most garbage found in landfills can be reused or recycled and often takes many, many years to break down. With all of the garbage thrown away each year, our landfills are quickly filling up. Help reduce the amount of trash that is thrown away by sorting your waste correctly.

Equipment

- A variety of recyclable materials (e.g., water bottles, newspapers, aluminum cans, plastic containers) or a variety of equipment (e.g., beanbags, skipping ropes, balls, scoops), enough for 2 items per student
- 5 or 6 recycling bins

Setup

- Line up each team in single-file formation behind a starting line, facing a pile of recyclable items on the other side of the gym.
- Place a recycling bin beside each team's start line.

How to Play

1. Divide players into five or six teams.
2. The first player runs to the recyclable pile, picks up one item, and runs back to drop it into his or her recycling bin and tags the next player in line. If players drop an item, they must pick it up before continuing.
3. The second player runs to the recyclable pile, picks up one item, and runs back to drop it into the recycling bin and tags the next player in line.
4. Continue until all items have been picked up and recycled.
5. Teams must sit quietly in a line, one behind the other, when finished.
6. The first team to finish recycling receives a high five from you.
7. All other teams may high-five each other for a recycling job well done.

Note

Ensure recyclable items are safe and clean.

Variations

- Before play begins, you may select how teams can win (e.g., the team who is the fastest, the team who runs the relay correctly, the team who encourages and cheers each other).

- Teams compete to see who can pick up the most recyclable items in a set time.

EVERY LITTLE BIT COUNTS

Eco Thought

Remind others to recycle their water bottles and plastic containers and to save their food scraps for composting. Encourage family and friends to buy items that can be recycled or are made from environmentally friendly materials, because every little bit counts!

Equipment

- Chart paper
- Markers
- Blank index cards
- Stopwatch or gym clock
- 8 plastic hoops (in 2 different colors to represent recycling centers and compost bins)

Setup

- Before class time, brainstorm a list of items that can be recycled and composted and write it on the chart paper.
- Use those ideas to create word cards. Write the name of one item on each index card. Try to create an equal number of cards for recyclable items and for compostable items. Create four word cards per student.
- Place the word cards in the middle of the gym or playing area.
- Place two plastic hoops in each corner of the playing area.
- Divide the players into eight teams (two teams in each corner).

How to Play

1. Each team sits around its plastic hoops (one recycling bin and one compost bin).
2. On the go signal, one player from each team jumps up, runs to the center, grabs one word card, and races back to place it in the appropriate hoop (e.g., a water bottle word card would go in the recycling bin hoop while a banana peel word card would go in the compost bin hoop).
3. That same player then taps the toe of the next player in the group, who jumps up, runs to the center, and retrieves another word card to place into the green depot.
4. Continue until the teams have been playing for 2-3 minutes.
5. Once time is called, each team counts the number of word cards it collected.

Notes

- Remind players that they may only pick up one word card at a time.
- Spread out word cards to prevent collisions.
- Encourage students to create their own word cards, including pictures.

Variations

- Challenge players by including word cards of items that cannot be recycled or composted and have them sort and categorize the photos and word cards when time is up.
- All players may run at the same time to collect word cards.

PITCH IN

Eco Thought

Recycling can be easy when we all pitch in and do it together. Find out how you can get recycling bins at your school and set up a recycling program. Recycling is good for all of us.

Equipment

- A variety of recyclable materials (e.g., water bottles, newspapers, aluminum cans, plastic containers) or a variety of equipment (e.g., beanbags, skipping ropes, balls, scoops), enough for 2 items per student
- 2 recycling bins
- Stopwatch or gym clock

Setup

- Divide players into two teams, forming two lines.
- Place an empty recycling bin at the end of each line and half of the recycling items at the beginning of each line.

How to Play

1. On the go signal, both teams pass their recycling items down their line.
2. The first player passes the item over his or her head to the second player, who passes it through his or her legs to the third player, who passes it over his or her head, and so on.
3. The first team to safely recycle all of its materials can cheer, "We pitched in!"

Note

Ensure recyclable items are safe and clean.

Variations

- Change the method of passing the recyclable items (e.g., elbows only, knees only, feet only, sideways).
- Move the bin farther away so that the last player in line can pitch it into a recycling bin, using a different way of pitching it each time (e.g., with one hand, overhand, underhand, set shot, with both feet, backward).

- Challenge the teams to see who can put the most recyclable materials into their bin within a set amount of time.
- Challenge the teams to beat their score within a set time.

TAKE CARE OF THE EARTH

Eco Thought

If you take care of the earth, the earth will take care of you. Treat the earth gently each day by reducing, reusing, recycling, and composting. What are some ways that you take care of the earth?

Equipment

2 soft medium-sized balls that represent the earth

Setup

- Divide players into two teams.
- Arrange each team into a line. Each player lies so that his or her head is near the next player's feet. This should space the players about three feet (1 m) apart.
- Once the players are spaced, have them sit up.

How to Play

1. The first player on each team grips the earth (a medium-sized ball) between his or her feet.
2. On the go signal, the first player rocks onto his or her back, passing the earth over the head with the feet to the next player in line behind him or her.
3. The second player grips the earth between his or her feet, rocks onto the back, and passes it over the head to the next player.
4. Continue passing the earth in this way to the last player.
5. When the last player has the earth, all players turn around and begin to pass the earth back down the line.

Note

Players do their best to take care of the earth by not dropping it.

STEP UP TO RECYCLING

Eco Thought

Step up by getting involved. Starting simple green initiatives at your school can go a long way to inspiring others. Bring a litterless lunch to school, turn off the lights when you leave your classroom, and use both sides of the paper before recycling. It all begins with you.

Equipment

- A variety of recyclable materials (e.g., water bottles, newspapers, aluminum cans, plastic containers) or a variety of equipment (e.g., beanbags, skipping ropes, balls, scoops), enough for 2 items per student
- 2 recycling bins

Setup

- Divide players into two teams.
- Line up each team so that partners sit toe to toe with knees bent.
- Place one bin with all the recyclables in it at one end of the line and the other bin empty at the other end of the line.

How to Play

1. On the go signal, the first pair picks up one of the recyclable items from the bin and works together to pass it with their feet to the next pair in line beside them.
2. The second pair passes the recyclable item with their feet to the next pair in line.
3. Continue passing the recyclable item this way until it reaches the last pair, who drop it into the recyclable bin at the end of the line with their feet.
4. Challenge the teams to see who can put the most recyclable materials into their bin within a set amount of time or to see which team can get all their recyclables into their bin the fastest.

Notes

- If players drop an item, they must find a way to pick it up with their feet and continue passing it.
- Ensure recyclable items are safe and clean

Variation

Challenge the teams to find creative ways to pass the recyclable items down the line (e.g., using elbows, knees, feet in the air).

THREE CHEERS FOR PLANET EARTH

Eco Thought

Helping the earth means making better choices. Reduce and produce less garbage. Reuse and find new uses for items. Recycle and save the earth's resources. Think of an everyday item that you use that can be reused in a different way.

Equipment

- 1 set of flags or signs attached to broom handles, each with a different environmental message per team:
  - Reduce what you use.
  - Reuse what you can.
  - Recycle the rest.
  - Three cheers for planet Earth!
- 1 pylon with a hole in the top for each flag

Setup

- Create four flags on broom handles for each of the groups.
- Divide the students into groups of four.
- Provide each group with a set of flags.
- Evenly space pylons along the length of the gym, approximately 15 feet (5 m) apart.

How to Play

1. Player 1 runs with the first flag (Reduce what you use.), places it in the first pylon, and runs back and tags player 2.
2. Player 2 runs with the second flag (Reuse what you can.), places it in the second pylon, and runs back and tags player 3.
3. Player 3 runs with the third flag (Recycle the rest.), places it in the third pylon, and runs back and tags player 4.
4. Player 4 runs with the fourth flag (Three cheers for planet Earth!), places it in the fourth pylon, and runs back.
5. Once the relay is completed, team members high-five each other and give three cheers for planet Earth.

Note

Challenge students to come up with their own environmental messages on the flags and a final cheer.

Variation

Once completed, continue the relay by removing the flags and bringing them back to the start line in reverse order.

CHAPTER

CIRCUIT AND STATION ACTIVITIES

Unless someone like you cares a whole awful lot, nothing is going to get better. It's not.

—Dr. Seuss, *The Lorax*

Circuit activities are easy to follow, keep students moving, and improve overall fitness. The circuit stations target muscular strength and endurance, skill development, and aerobic activities. Students work in small groups and travel from one station to another every few minutes (2-5 minutes at each station depending on age, grade level, and ability). By incorporating the three Rs into the circuits, we help improve the overall health of the planet.

TRASH BALL FITNESS

Eco Thought

Reusing paper helps to save many trees from being cut down to make new paper. Use both sides and the whole piece of paper before putting it in the recycling bin. How many ways can paper be reused?

Equipment

- 1 bin of recycled paper for each student (use different colors at each station)
- 6 baskets per station
- 1 basketball hoop
- 8 pylons
- Music

Setup

- Students use crumpled paper to perform the trash ball fitness circuit.
- Students perform the activity at each station and rotate when time is called or music stops.

How to Play

Station 1: Tricks

Toss and catch a crumpled-paper ball using a variety of methods (e.g., over the shoulder, under a leg, behind the back, figure eights).

Station 2: Shoot Hoops

1. Use a crumpled-paper ball to practice taking shots into a basketball hoop.
2. Challenge yourself by standing farther away.

Station 3: Crumpled Crunches

1. Sit toe to toe with a partner, knees bent, feet flat.
2. Lie down and then sit up to meet your partner in the middle.
3. Pass the crumpled-paper ball every time you meet.

Station 4: Fitness Challenge

1. Place pylons and paper balls at each end of the gym.
2. Run to one pylon and pick up a crumpled-paper ball.
3. Run back and drop it off, exchanging it for another one.
4. Continue to run back, drop it off, and exchange it for another one.

Station 5: Bocce Ball

1. Throw out a white crumpled-paper ball as your target ball.
2. Everyone chooses a color for his or her crumpled-paper bocce ball.
3. Everyone takes a turn throwing a paper bocce ball, trying to land it as close to the target as possible.
4. Use an underhand throw, overhand throw, right arm, or left arm.

Station 6: Foot Hockey

1. Divide into two groups.
2. Use pylons to create two goal areas approximately 15 feet (4.5 meters) apart and a crumpled-paper ball.

Note

Invite students to create their own fitness circuit using recycled paper.

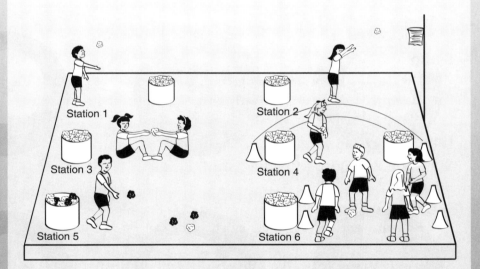

Eco Thought

Healthy active living takes on a new meaning when we take a second look at items and find new ways to be active using old stuff. Taking small steps to reuse simple items is a great way to help save the earth's resources and keep the earth healthy. Can you think of items that can be used to create new games?

Equipment

- Music
- 4 sets of large plastic soda pop bottles (6 bottles per set)
- Socks, recycled paper, or yarn balls, 3 per student
- 1 tennis racket (made with a wire hanger and pair of nylons) per student at the station
- 1 to 4 recycling bins
- Hand towels or dish towels, 1 per student at the station

Setup

- Divide the students into four groups.
- Have students perform the activity at each station and rotate when time is called or music stops.

How to Play

Station 1: Pop Bottle Bowling

Setup

- Set up the large plastic soda pop bottles as bowling pins.
- Roll up a pair of socks to use as a bowling ball.

Activity

Students use the sock ball to knock down the bottles. Each student should take three turns bowling, then reset the pins for the next player.

Station 2: Hanger Tennis

Setup

- Bend the wire coat hanger into a diamond shape to create a tennis racquet and pull one leg of the nylons over it to create a small tennis racket.
- Roll up one sock to make a small, light ball.

Activity

Students try the following challenges:

- Keep the ball in the air by bouncing it on the racket.
- With a friend, keep the ball in the air by hitting it back and forth to each other.
- Count the number of times you can bounce the ball without dropping it. Start counting again from zero if you drop the ball.

Station 3: Sock Ball Basketball

Setup

Place a recycling bin at the station and roll up a pair of socks to use as a ball.

Activity

Students perform a set shot by shooting the sock ball into the recycling bin. Students may increase the challenge by placing the box farther away from the starting point. They also may set up a basketball game by passing the sock and shooting it into the bin.

Station 4: Sock Towel Toss

Setup

Provide hand towels or dish towels to each student along with balls made of socks, recycled paper, or yarn.

Activity

Hold a small towel at each end, fold it in, and snap it out to toss a rolled-up sock into the air and catch. Practice passing the rolled-up sock back and forth to a friend.

SCHOOL YARD FITNESS

Eco Thought

Take a moment to get to know your school yard and get active outdoors. Go for a walk, play a game of tag, or play a game of hide-and-seek using trees. Get outside and play with your family and friends and reconnect with nature.

Equipment

- 8 pylons
- 8 activity cards (made from index cards)

Setup

- Make cards with descriptions of activities to be performed at each station.
- Divide students into eight groups.
- Spread out the circuit activities around the playing area.
- Place one pylon and one activity card at each station.
- Start each group at a different activity station.
- Rotate groups clockwise around the circuit when time is called.

How to Play

Activity 1: Jog to a tree, a fence, and a swing. Tap each one with your thumb.

Activity 2: Squat in a single-file line. The last player in the line leapfrogs over the other players and squats at the front of the line. The person who is now last in the line leapfrogs over the players and begins the pattern again. Players should continue until time is called.

Activity 3: Do eight curl-ups at three different trees.

Activity 4: Hop from one soccer goal post to the other and back.

Activity 5: Scoot under and around five different playground objects (e.g., slide, swing, recycling bin, garbage can).

Activity 6: Run once around the perimeter of the playground.

Activity 7: Skip to a wall of the school and perform a wall-sit for 10 seconds.

Activity 8: Do three star jumps beside the tallest tree on the playground.

Note

Invite students to create their own outdoor activity and try it out.

ECO OLYMPICS

Eco Thought

You don't have to be an Olympian to help the earth. Find new and creative ways to reuse items in your quest to have fun, get fit, and be healthy. Go for gold and go green!

Equipment

- Colored recycled paper, 3 pieces per student
- Pylons
- Beanbags in different colors, 3 per student
- Music

Setup

- Divide students into five groups.
- Have students perform the track and field events at each station using recycled paper materials and rotate when time is called or music stops.

How to Play

Station 1: Shot put

Activity

1. Mark a starting line with pylons.
2. Choose a colored piece of paper for your shot put; each student selects a different color.
3. Crumple the paper into a ball.
4. Throw the shot put as far as you can.
5. Have a friend mark your distance with a beanbag.
6. Try it three times, then switch.

Station 2: Discus

Equipment

- 3 paper plates or pieces of cardboard per student
- 2 pylons
- 3 beanbags per student

Activity

1. Mark a starting line with pylons.
2. Choose a paper plate for your discus.

(continued)

3. Hold the paper plate like a Frisbee and throw it as far as you can.
4. Have a friend mark your distance with a beanbag.
5. Try it three times, then switch.

Station 3: Javelin

Equipment

- 3 poster rolls or wrapping-paper rolls per student
- 3 pylons per student
- 3 beanbags per student

Activity

1. Mark a starting line with pylons.
2. Choose a paper roll for your javelin.
3. Take one step forward and launch the javelin with an overhand throw.
4. Have a friend mark your distance with a beanbag.
5. Try it three times, then switch.

Station 4: Relay

Equipment

- 1 toilet paper or paper towel roll per team
- 4 pylons

Activity

1. Use pylons to mark the start–finish line for the course.
2. Spread out the members of your group around the perimeter of the gym or playground, all runners an equal distance apart.
3. Choose a paper towel roll to use as a baton.
4. The first runner begins at the starting line, runs with the baton, and passes it to the second runner.
5. The second student runs and passes the baton to the third runner.
6. The third student runs and passes the baton to the fourth runner.
7. The fourth student runs with the baton to the finish line.
8. Run again, switching running positions.

Station 5: Hurdles

Equipment

- 6 poster or wrapping-paper rolls
- 16 pylons

Activity

1. Use four pylons to mark a start line and a finish line for the course.
2. Set up six hurdles an equal distance apart. Create a hurdle using two pylons and a paper roll.
3. Begin at the start line and jump over the hurdles.
4. When one student reaches the halfway mark, the next student should start.

Eco Thought

Reducing energy is an important way to help conserve the earth's resources. Can you think of ways to save energy? Try turning off the lights, hanging laundry outside instead of using a dryer, or using a bike instead of getting a ride.

Equipment

Music

Setup

- Divide the students into six groups.
- Start each group at one of the stations and have them perform the activity for approximately one minute.
- Rotate students from station to station.

How to Play

Station 1: Hang up the laundry

Equipment

- 1 long skipping rope attached to a wall using tape
- 1 basket of clothespins and pieces of cloth, towels, or recycled paper

Activity

Students bend down to pick up the laundry and clothespins and hang it on the skipping rope.

Note

If the equipment is not available, students should pretend to hang up the laundry by touching their toes and reaching up to hang it continuously until time is up.

Station 2: Pedal power

Equipment

- 2 chairs for every 3 students

Activity

1. One student stands between the two back-to-back chairs.
2. Two students sit in the chairs for safety and support.
3. The first student places his or her hands on the back of the chairs for support, raises his or her legs, and begins pedaling as if riding a bike.

Note

If chairs are not available, students may lie on their backs and cycle legs in the air.

Station 3: Trash-ball tricks

Equipment

3 crumpled-paper balls per student

Activity

Students toss and catch paper balls over the shoulder, under a leg, behind the back, and so on.

Station 4: Step up your recycling

Equipment

1 bench

Activity

1. Students step up on the bench one foot at a time.
2. Students step down from the bench one foot at a time.
3. Foot pattern is up, up, down, down.

Note

Students must step up with their full foot on the bench for safety.

Station 5: Trash-ball targets

Equipment

- 3 crumpled-paper balls per student
- 3 or 4 garbage bins, recycling bins, or basketball hoops (use bins of various heights and sizes)
- 3 or 4 pylons

Activity

1. Students shoot hoops with recycled-paper balls.
2. Challenge students to hit a variety of bins.
3. Challenge students to shoot from various distances, using pylons as markers.

Station 6: Make a wish for the earth

Equipment

- 1 bucket or recycling bin
- 10 coins per student

Activity

1. Place a bucket in the middle of a circle in the gym.

(continued)

2. Arrange students in a circle around the bucket.
3. Provide each student with 10 coins.
4. On the go signal, have students toss coins one at a time underhand into the bucket.
5. Each coin represents a wish for the earth.

Note

For safety, students may only retrieve coins when all players have finished tossing.

PLIGHT OF THE POLAR BEAR

Eco Thought

Polar bears are endangered because of the negative impact of global warming on their environment. Melting ice is causing the polar bears' habitat to disappear, making it hard for them to hunt and survive. The first step toward reducing our role in global warming is to learn how our actions might affect wildlife.

Equipment

- Music
- 14 large gym mats
- 14 pylons
- 1 ball for every 2 students in the group
- 3 beanbags for each student at one station
- 1 bench
- Minimum of 8 poly spots

Setup

- Divide the students into six groups.
- Students perform the activity at each station for one to two minutes and rotate when time is called or when the music stops.

How to Play

Station 1: Polar bear push-ups

Setup

Spread three of the large gym mats out in the station area.

Activity

1. Perform push-ups.
2. Perform a combination of wall, floor, or modified (knee) push-ups.
3. See how many you can do until time is called.

Station 2: Arctic swim

Setup

Use the 8 pylons to designate the jogging lane.

Activity

1. *Swim* (jog) around the perimeter of the gym.
2. See how many laps you can do before time is called.

(continued)

Station 3: Snowball sit-ups

Setup

Spread three of the large gym mats out in the station area.

Activity

1. Sit toe to toe with a partner, knees bent, feet flat.
2. Lie down and then sit up to meet each other in the middle.
3. Pass the snowball every time you meet.

Station 4: Seal search and rescue

Setup

- Set up the pylons in a zigzag pattern.
- Place the beanbags at one end of the pylon pattern.
- Stand three of the gym mats on their sides to create a cave.

Activity

1. Bear-walk in a zigzag pattern through the snow drifts (pylons).
2. Pick up one seal (beanbag).
3. Crawl back through the snowy cave.
4. Continue searching.

Station 5: Iceberg

Setup

- To create an incline, stack a few mats on top of each other with another mat at the bottom of the incline for safety.
- Place the bench next to one of the mats flat on the floor.

Activity

1. Log roll down the iceberg (inclined mat) and onto the snow (flat mat).
2. Crawl across the tundra (bench), jump off, and land onto the snow (mat).
3. Bear-walk back to start.

Station 6: Crossing the ice floes

Setup

Place the poly spots in a random pattern.

Activity

1. Using a one-foot (0.3 m) take-off, leap across the ice floes (poly spots).
2. Run back to start.

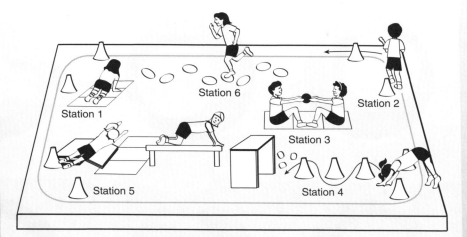

CHAPTER

4

LITERACY AND DRAMA ACTIVITIES

Tell me, I forget. Show me, I remember. Involve me, I understand.

—Ancient Chinese proverb

The activities in this chapter engage the mind and body by allowing students to think while being active. These literacy and drama activities encourage students to be active and to think about the way we treat Mother Earth and improve self-confidence. Creating a healthy mind, a healthy body, and a healthy world can be possible when we make green choices.

ENVIRONMENTAL CROSSWORDS

Eco Thought

We all play a part in protecting our natural environment. We can put the green pieces together by taking an active role in building a healthy world for humans and wildlife. What are some ways that we can build a greener world? Composting, conserving energy, and using the three Rs are just the start of making a difference.

Equipment

3 or 4 sets of alphabet beanbags or letters of the alphabet written on paper

Setup

- To introduce this game, brainstorm a list of words with an environmental focus (e.g., recycle, compost, reduce, ecology, green, conservation, energy).
- Model an example of a crossword puzzle using the beanbags.
- Place students into groups of four, numbering each member 1 to 4.
- Place the letter beanbags in the middle of the playing area.
- Scatter the groups around the perimeter of the playing area.

How to Play

1. As a group, students choose a word from the environmental list to spell.
2. The first student must move by walking or hopping or something else to the middle of the playing area and retrieve one beanbag.
3. Upon returning to the group, the student drops off the beanbag and high-fives the next student, who then moves in a different way to retrieve another letter.
4. Once the first word is completed, students begin to retrieve letters for the next word from the list.
5. Challenge each group to come up with three to five words in their puzzle.

Note

Check for accurate spelling.

Variations

- Choose an environmental theme, such as energy conservation, recycling, endangered animals, and generate a new list of words.
- Challenge students to play the game without brainstorming a list.

HEALTHY-ENVIRONMENT CHARADES

Eco Thought

By using the three Rs we can help maintain a healthy environment. Reduce, reuse, and recycle all depend on each other to make a difference in reducing pollution and waste in our world. Together we can make a difference!

Equipment

- 4 environmental charade cards
- 1 garbage can
- 4 recycling bins

Setup

- Divide students into four groups.
- Create an environmental charade card for each of the following:
  - Activity 1
    1. Shuffle sideways for the length of the gym.
    2. Once there, jump up and down three times and say, "Reduce, reuse, recycle rocks!"
  - Activity 2
    1. Run to each corner of the gym or playing area.
    2. Pretend to pick up an item to be recycled by tapping the recycling bin.
    3. Use arms to swim to the centre of the playing area.
    4. Sit down in a straight line and row your boat.
  - Activity 3
    1. Skip to each circle on the gym floor.
    2. Pretend to turn off the bathroom taps.
    3. Run to a side wall of the gym and pretend to rock climb.
    4. Perform a wall-sit against the wall.
  - Activity 4
    1. Pretend to pick up litter in the middle of the playing area.
    2. Run it over to a garbage bin located by one of the exit doors.
    3. Bum-walk to the closest line on the floor.
    4. High-five each group member.

How to Play

1. Invite one student from each group to come up and read an activity card.
2. After reading the environmental charade card, the student runs back to his or her group and shares the information.
3. Each group performs the actions in order as stated on the environmental charade card.
4. While the students are completing the task, the teacher checks that the actions are completed in the correct order.
5. Continue playing until all students have had a chance to come up and read an environmental charade card.

Variations

- Students try the activity without speaking.
- Students create their own environmental charade cards and try them out.

Eco Thought

When was the last time you enjoyed the outdoors? Take a moment and go for a hike with your friends and family, taking in all of the sights and sounds of nature!

Equipment

- Chart paper or chalkboard
- Music

Setup

- Post the list of healthy environmental actions.
- Students scatter around the playing area.

Walk to a park—March in place.

Climb a mountain—Alternate lifting one knee high and reaching up with the opposite arm.

Paddle a canoe—Squat and paddle three times to the right and three times to the left.

Fly a kite—Run the length of the gym, holding arms in the air.

Apply sunscreen and rub it in.

Row your boat—Sit down, knees bent, facing a partner. Hold partner's hands and row back and forth five times.

Ride a bike—Lie on your back and pedal feet in the air six times.

Go for a hike—Walk briskly with arms pumping around the perimeter of the playing area.

How to Play

1. Call out the actions to be performed on the spot.
2. Change actions every 5 to 10 seconds.

Variations

- Choose a student leader to call out the actions.
- Challenge students by increasing the intensity, speed, and repetitions of the movements.
- With the class, brainstorm a new list of actions related to a different environmental theme and try them out.

PUT YOUR BEST FOOT FORWARD

Eco Thought

Are you doing your part to help the environment? It can be as simple as reducing your waste, recycling items, or reusing something instead of just throwing it out. Taking one step at a time will help save our planet.

Equipment

List of questions pertaining to the environment

Do you compost your food scraps?

Do you recycle newspapers?

Have you planted a vegetable garden at your home?

Have you hugged a tree lately?

Have you ever planted a tree?

Do you walk to the store instead of driving?

Do you walk to school instead of getting a ride?

Do you use reusable containers for your lunch?

Do you recycle your clothes to someone in need?

Do you turn the water off when you brush your teeth?

Do you take your own bags to the store when you go shopping?

Do you unplug your electronics when not in use?

Do you turn off the lights when you leave the room?

Do you use a clothesline instead of the dryer?

Setup

Students stand in a line across the width of the gym or playing area.

How to Play

1. Ask a question on the subject of the environment and include an action for students to perform depending on their answer (e.g., Hop forward if you recycle).
2. If the student answers yes, the student moves forward.
3. Students move forward by taking a giant step, hopping, jumping, leaping, taking a side-step, and so on.
4. If the student answers no, he or she remains in the same spot.

Variation

Students create their own questions concerning the environment.

Eco Thought

Imagine what you can do! The choices that you make each day can have a huge impact on a greener future. By making smart choices, you and your family can help keep our air and water clean and our environment healthy. Get into the habit of biking or walking to school or bringing a litterless lunch and a reusable water bottle.

Equipment

Chart paper

Setup

Chart the following phrases.

Example: If I were a bird, I could . . . [fly through the sky]

If I were a flower, I could . . .

If I were a tree, I could . . .

If I were a frog, I could . . .

If I were a plastic container, I could be made into a new . . .

If I were a bear, I would . . .

If I were a newspaper, I would . . .

If I were an old pair of jeans, I could be made into . . .

If I were a seed, I could grow into a . . .

If I were an aluminum can, I could . . .

If I were a glass bottle, I could . . .

If I were a cardboard box, I could . . .

How to Play

1. Call out the phrases.
2. Students complete the phrases by dramatizing their answers.

Variation

Have students create their own ideas to dramatize.

CAN YOU . . . ?

Eco Thought

Are there animals at risk in your community? Can you imagine a world without animals? Our actions can have a huge impact on wildlife and their habitat. Help protect plants and animals before they become endangered or disappear altogether.

Equipment

None

How to Play

1. Call out the following animal movement questions.
2. Students perform the actions continuously until the next question is asked.

Can you bound like a deer?
Can you run like a spider?
Can you crawl like a snake?
Can you fly like a bird?
Can you walk like a penguin?
Can you swim like a fish?
Can you waddle like a duck?
Can you scurry like a mouse?
Can you hop like a frog?
Can you gallop like a horse?
Can you walk like a crab?
Can you lumber like a bear?

Variations

- Introduce to the list items that you can recycle:
  - Can you roll like a tin can?
  - Can you crumple like recycled paper?
  - Can you squash down like a plastic bottle?
  - Can you flatten like a stack of newspaper?
- Have students create their own ways to move.

ON THE MOVE WITH ENDANGERED ANIMALS

Eco Thoughts

We share the planet with millions of animals, insects, and birds, many of which are endangered. By using the three Rs, we can reduce the negative impact on our natural environment. When exploring nature, show respect by staying on paths and trails and taking waste and recyclables home.

Equipment

None

How to Play

1. Call out the actions for each endangered animal for students to perform as they move throughout the gym:
   - Polar bear – Move on hands and feet, keeping arms and legs stiff.
   - Frog – Hop on all fours.
   - Seal – In a push-up position, use arms only to move and drag feet behind.
   - Gorilla – Slowly walk in a low position, with hands sweeping the ground.
   - Elephant – Walk, leaning forward with one arm swaying like a trunk.
   - Eagle – Fly with outstretched arms.
   - Cheetah – Run around the perimeter of the gym.
   - Alligator – Walk with extended arms opening and closing like jaws.
2. Students perform the actions continuously until the next animal is called.

Variation

Challenge your students to identify other endangered animals and come up with an action.

Polar bear   Seal   Elephant   Eagle   Alligator

Eco Thought

By recognizing the value of our natural environment, we can find ways to protect it and maintain a healthy world for us all. What are you doing to help protect the environment?

Equipment

None

How to Play

1. Call out the environmental actions and corresponding activities for students to perform in the classroom.
   - If you turn off the lights when you leave a room, skip around your desk (or pylon) two times.
   - If you brought a litterless lunch, reach for the sky and clap your hands three times.
   - If you turn off the taps while brushing your teeth, power jump three times.
   - If you like to take nature hikes, jump up and touch a high spot on the wall three times.
   - If you ride your bike, do 10 wall push-ups.
   - If you recycle pop bottles, hop on one foot for five seconds then switch feet.
   - If you compost, grapevine to the right and clap, then grapevine to the left and clap.
   - If you take along a cloth bag when you shop, do alternating knee lifts for 10 seconds.
   - If you reuse gift bags, do five jumping jacks.
   - If your family celebrates Earth Day, star jump and shout "Hooray!"
2. Students perform the actions continuously until the next action is called.

Note

Have students come up with their own ideas.

CHAPTER

FITNESS ACTIVITIES

It's not easy being green!

—Kermit the Frog

Our fitness activities allow students to exercise their entire body through physical challenges. By keeping students moving, these activities strengthen heart and lungs, build muscle, and increase flexibility. Exercising is energizing. Reenergize the earth!

WHOLE WORLD IN YOUR HANDS

Eco Thought

One simple day of action can have a huge impact on the health and well-being of the planet. Each of us has a hand in the future of our world, and together we can make a difference. Take responsibility for your actions and find ways to make a positive impact on the earth. What little green deed can you do?

Equipment

- 1 medium-sized ball per student
- Music

How to Play

Students perform the following exercises for a count of 8, 10, or 12 seconds or for 8, 10, or 12 reps, depending on the activity.

- Earth walk: Walk around the gym holding the ball in front.
- Around the world:
  - Place the ball at your feet.
  - Stand with feet shoulder-width apart and knees slightly bent.
  - Pick up the ball, reach out to the side, extend ball overhead and back to the floor in a circular motion, and repeat.
  - Change directions.
- Keeping the world strong:
  - Start with feet shoulder-width apart and knees slightly bent.
  - Hold the ball against the wall, step away from the wall and perform a push-up with hands on the ball at chest level, and repeat.
- Take care of the earth:
  - Start with feet shoulder-width apart and knees slightly bent.
  - Stand close to the wall and hold the ball against the wall at chest level.
  - Walk the ball up the wall with fingertips and hold the stretch at the top.
  - Walk the ball back down the wall, and repeat.
- Earth rotation:
  - Start with feet shoulder-width apart, and knees slightly bent.
  - Hold the ball out in front, twist at the waist to the left, and return to the center.

- o Twist at the waist to the right and return to center.
- o Repeat sequence.
- Earth-sit:
  - o Start with feet shoulder-width apart and knees slightly bent.
  - o With arms extended holding the ball, perform a squat and return to standing position.
  - o Variation: Raise ball over head.
- Lifting the earth:
  - o Place feet shoulder-width apart with ball on the ground.
  - o Starting on the right side, bend down to pick up the ball and reach up diagonally to the left side.
  - o Repeat action on the opposite side.
- Hug the earth:
  - o Place feet shoulder-width apart.
  - o With knees slightly bent, extend the ball with outstretched arms.
  - o Hold and pull it in to hug the ball.
  - o Variation: Balance on one foot.
  - o Variation: Balance on one foot and extend the other leg outward.
- Supporting the earth:
  - o Place the ball behind you in the small of your back and lean against the wall.
  - o Squat with arms extended and hold the position for three to five seconds.
  - o Return to starting position.

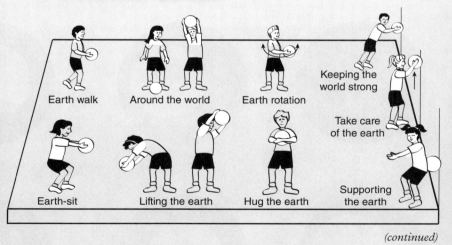

Earth walk   Around the world   Earth rotation   Keeping the world strong

Earth-sit   Lifting the earth   Hug the earth   Take care of the earth   Supporting the earth

(continued)

Notes

- All ball activities may be performed against a wall for extra support.
- All of these activities can easily become an exercise ball circuit.

Variation

Have students create their own moves.

PAPER-BALL FITNESS

Eco Thought

Recycling should become second nature, an automatic thing to do. And because even a little bit of food or drink can spoil the contents of the recycle bin, be sure to rinse out items before you toss them in. Keep it clean!

Equipment

1 recycled piece of paper with a physical activity written on it per student

Setup

- Provide each student with a piece of recycled paper with a fitness activity written on it.
- Students crumple the paper and toss it anywhere in the gym.

How to Play

1. Students run, skip, gallop, or hop around the gym. On the signal "recycle," students pick up a paper ball, open it, and perform the fitness activity.
2. Once completed, students crumple up the paper and toss it anywhere in the gym again.
3. Repeat the activity.

Variations

- Place a recycling bin in the middle of the playing area and have players toss the paper balls in the bin after they have completed their fitness activity.
- Students toss and catch the recycled paper with a partner. On the signal "recycle," players open the crumpled paper and perform the fitness activity.

BACK TO NATURE

Eco Thought

Connecting with nature is good for our well-being. Enjoying fresh air, exercise, and the peacefulness of nature has the power to make you feel healthier and happier. Take your family for a walk in the great outdoors and enjoy nature's gifts. What are ways you can enjoy nature with your family?

Equipment

- 1 chair per student
- Music

How to Play

Have students perform the following activities while seated.

- A breath of fresh air:
  - Reach up to the sky, breathing in through your nose.
  - Bring arms down, breathing out through your mouth.
  - Repeat.
- Walk in the woods:
  - March on the spot.
  - Swing bent arms forward and back.
- Canoe: Paddle the canoe for six strokes on each side.
- Portage:
  - While marching on the spot, pick up a canoe and raise it overhead with arms stretched out.
  - Every three seconds, bend arms and raise canoe again.
- Mountain climbing:
  - Reach up to the sky with alternating arms.
  - March on the spot with high knees.
- Biking: Hold the sides of the chair while pedaling feet in a forward motion or pedal backward.
- Swim in the lake:
  - Perform the front crawl, alternating arms.
  - Flutter kick your feet.

- Tread water:
  - Hold arms out to the sides and rotate them like you're treading water.
  - Raise knees and rotate feet in a circular motion like an eggbeater.
- Pick berries:
  - Reach up with left arm to pick a berry.
  - Reach down and place it in the basket on right side.
  - Switch sides.
- Lie in the sun:
  - Perform a full-body stretch by stretching the arms overhead and legs straight out.
  - Hold for three seconds.
  - Relax, then stretch again.

Variation

Have students create their own actions.

Adapted from The Toronto Board.

REEEUSE! REEECYCLE!

Eco Thought

Whether you recycle an item to make something new or if you reuse an item for another purpose, you are saving energy, water, and landfill space and reducing pollution.

Equipment

Pylons

Setup

- Divide the class into two groups: reuse and recycle.
- Establish a safety zone on each end of the gym or playing area for each group.
- If the class is outside, use pylons to create a centerline.

How to Play

1. Students line up three giant steps away from the centerline facing each other.
2. Teacher calls out either Reeeuse! or Reeecycle!
3. When the teacher calls out reuse, the reuse students turn and run back to their safety line while the recycle students chase them.
4. When the teacher calls out recycle, the recycle students turn and run back to their safety line while the reuse students chase them.
5. The chasing team tries to tag as many students on the back or shoulders as possible.
6. If tagged, that student becomes a member of the other group and play resumes.

Note

Ensure that the safety line is approximately three giant steps away from the end walls.

TAKE A PASS ON POLLUTION

Eco Thought

Almost all pollution on earth is manmade. Pollution affects air, water, and soil and can cause sickness in humans, wildlife, and our natural environment. We can help to reduce pollution by making a better effort to include the three Rs in our daily lives.

Equipment

- 1 deck of cards
- Chart paper or chalkboard
- Music

Setup

On chart paper, list the following environmental fitness activities.

Ace: Reach up to pick an apple.

King: Side lunge and pull out the weeds.

Queen: Dig the earth with a shovel.

Jack: Raise the roof by raising your arms on both sides.

10: Ski hop over a line.

9: Wiggle on the spot like a worm.

8: Power jump up and say, "Go green."

7: Jump and twist while picking up litter.

6: Jog around the gym.

5: Lie down and make snow angels.

4: Jump and tap a tree branch.

3: Lunge walk around the room.

2: Hug yourself for going green.

How to Play

1. The teacher hands out one card to each student.
2. Students perform the fitness activity specified by the card they are holding. Students perform the exercise for 8, 10, or 12 seconds or 8, 10, or 12 reps, depending on the activity.
3. Upon completion, students walk throughout the area, exchanging cards with other students.
4. When the dealer announces, "Go green," students stop and perform the fitness activity on their current card.
5. Once the activity is completed, students exchange cards again.

Adapted, by permission, from Peel District School Board, 2006, *Hooked on DPA-Daily physical activity* (Mississauga, ON: Peel District School Board).

DON'T BE A LITTER BUG!

Eco Thought

Take a moment to help clean up our earth by putting trash in its place. Litter makes our parks unsafe and endangers the lives of animals. Use a garbage bin for items that cannot be reused or recycled. Keep our parks clean. Litter not!

Equipment

- Beanbags (minimum of 100)
- 1 garbage can per group

Setup

- Place a pile of litter (beanbags) in the middle of the playing area.
- Divide the class into two groups.
- Place one garbage can in each group's end zone.
- Have groups start in their end zone.

How to Play

1. On the signal, "Clean up," everyone runs to the pile of litter and picks up one beanbag.
2. Students run with the beanbags to their end zone and place them in the garbage can.
3. Students run back to the litter pile and repeat the action.
4. When time is called, the teacher asks each group to count how much litter they picked up.

Notes

- Students may only take one beanbag at a time.
- Students must *place* the beanbag in the garbage can, not throw it.

Variations

- Place several small trash bins in each team's playing area.
- Challenge each team to beat their score.

REDUCE, REUSE, RECYCLE CHALLENGE

Eco Thought

Challenge your friends and family members to reduce more, reuse more, and recycle more at home, school, and work. One easy idea is to take reusable cloth bags to the grocery store instead of using plastic bags. Can you think of other ways to use the three Rs?

Equipment

Chart paper or chalkboard

Setup

- Chart the reduce, reuse, and recycle headings with accompanying actions and rules of the game as listed in the how-to-play section.
- Divide the class into two groups.
- Establish a safety zone at each end of the gym or playing area.
- From the centerline in the gym or playing area, establish a 15-foot (about 5 m) start line for each group.

How to Play

1. Each group huddles in their safe zone and secretly chooses their R: reduce, reuse, or recycle.
2. Groups return to the middle of the playing area to stand on their start line facing each other.
3. On the signal "Go green," both groups show their chosen action at the same time:
   - Reduce—squat
   - Reuse—extend your arms and legs out in a star shape
   - Recycle—hug yourself
4. Depending on which action the groups show, students will either chase the other group, attempting to tag them before they reach the safe zone, or turn and run back to their own safe zone.
5. The rules of the game:
   - Reduce (squat) chases reuse (star).
   - Reuse (star) chases recycle (hug yourself).
   - Recycle (hug yourself) chases reduce (squat).
6. Once caught, that student becomes a member of the other group and play resumes.
7. If groups choose the same signal, they should select a different action and play again.

Note

Ensure the safety line is approximately three giant steps away from the end walls.

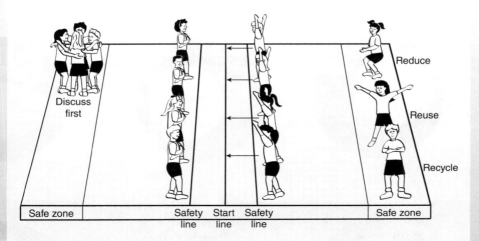

Adapted, by permission, from CIRA, 2003, Evolution. In *Why paper & scissors rock!!* (Ontario, Canada: Canadian Intramural Recreation Association of Ontario), 32.

GET OUTSIDE AND PLAY: WINTER FITNESS

Eco Thought

This winter, spend time outdoors trying a new activity with your family and friends. Create holiday cheer by encouraging your friends to go green with their celebrations and reduce holiday waste by doing things such as reusing gift bags for another occasion.

Equipment

- A minimum of 10 pieces of recycled paper with fitness activities written on them
- 1 recycling bin

Setup

- Prepare the physical fitness cards and place them in the recycling bin in the middle of the gym or playing area:
  - Brush the snow off the car: Stretch arm out and use a waving motion to brush the snow off; switch arms.
  - Shovel the walk: Bend knees and use a shoveling action with arms.
  - Build a snow person: Pretend to roll the snow creating the body of a snow person.
  - Make a snow angel:
    - Lie down with arms and legs extended.
    - Bring arms and legs in toward the body and back out continuously.
  - Throw a snowball: Pretend to pack snow in the shape of a ball and throw it overhand.
  - Ice skate on the pond: Using legs and arms in opposition, slide feet out to the side in a skating motion.
  - Cross-country ski: Using opposite arms and legs, slide forward with outstretched arms and legs in a skiing motion.
  - Hang a bird feeder:
    - Reach down and pick up the feeder.
    - Reach up to hang it in a tree.
    - Repeat.
  - Walk in the woods: March on the spot with high knees and arms swinging.

- Hibernate like a bear: Curl up in a ball and rock and roll.
- Students form a circle in the gym.

How to Play

1. One student runs in, retrieves a fitness card from the recycling bin and performs the fitness activity for 10 to 15 seconds or 10 to 15 reps, depending on the activity.
2. The class follows the student leader by performing the same fitness activity.
3. Students take turns choosing a fitness activity and leading an activity.

Variations

- Have students select a different method of locomotion each time to retrieve a fitness activity (e.g., walk in, skip in, run in, crab-walk in).
- Divide students into four groups and place them in the corners of the gym or playing area.
  - One student runs in, retrieves a fitness activity, and returns to the group.
  - The whole group performs the fitness activity together.
  - All group members have a chance to retrieve a fitness activity.
- Challenge students to create new fitness activities.
- Use fitness activity cards cut into seasonal shapes (e.g., leaf, flower, snowflake).

GET OUTSIDE AND PLAY: SPRING FITNESS

Eco Thought

This spring grow your own vegetables or plant flowers and enjoy the beauty of your gardens. Organize a community cleanup in the neighborhood park or get together with your neighbors and hold a garage sale.

Equipment

- A minimum of 10 pieces of recycled paper with fitness activities written on them
- 1 recycling bin

Setup

- Prepare the physical fitness cards and place them in the recycling bin in the middle of the gym or playing area:
  - Dig the dirt: Turn over the dirt using a shoveling action.
  - Plant seeds:
    - Bend down, place a seed, stamp it down with the foot.
    - Alternate hands and feet.
  - Weed: Bend knees and pull up the weeds.
  - Community clean-up:
    - Bend and reach to grab the litter.
    - Overhand toss it into the trash can.
  - Fertilize the lawn: Pivot on the spot, underhand tossing the fertilizer using alternating hands.
  - Water the garden:
    - Place one hand on hip, the other hand out to the side.
    - Move hand in a jerking motion across the body (to illustrate the movement of a sprinkler) and sweep arm back to starting point.
    - Switch hands.
  - Go for a spring walk: March on the spot.
  - Look for signs of spring:
    - Place one hand on hip and one hand shading eyes.
    - Twist at the trunk, looking side to side.
  - Bear walk: Walk on all fours, keeping arms straight, knees slightly bent, and bottom in the air.
  - Take out the outdoor toys:

- Skip to the center of the gym or playing area.
- Pretend to pick up a toy.
- Skip to a corner of the playing area to drop it off.
- Students form a circle in the gym or playing area.

How to Play

1. One student runs in, retrieves a fitness card from the recycling bin, and performs the fitness activity for 10 to 15 seconds or 10 to 15 reps, depending on the activity.
2. The class follows the student leader by performing the same fitness activity.
3. All students take turns choosing a fitness activity and leading it.

Variations

- Students select a different method of locomotion each time to retrieve a fitness activity (e.g., walk in, skip in, run in, crab-walk in).
- Divide students into four groups and place them in the corners of the gym or playing area.
  - One student runs in, retrieves a fitness activity, and returns to the group.
  - The whole group performs the fitness task together.
  - All group members have a chance to retrieve a fitness activity.
- Challenge students to create new fitness activities.
- Use fitness activity cards cut into seasonal shapes (e.g., leaf, flower, snowflake).

GET OUTSIDE AND PLAY: SUMMER FITNESS

Eco Thought

This summer enjoy what nature has to offer. Get outside with your family and friends: Go for a hike, visit a beach, enjoy an outdoor picnic!

Equipment

- A minimum of 10 pieces of recycled paper with fitness activities written on them
- 1 recycling bin

Setup

- Place the physical fitness cards in the recycling bin in the middle of the gym or playing area.
  - Walk in the park: March on the spot.
  - Swing on the swings:
    - Sit on bottom.
    - Pull knees into chest.
    - Rock back and forth.
  - Fly a kite: Jog with an arm up holding the string of the kite.
  - Look at the stars in the sky:
    - Place one hand on hip, one hand shading eyes.
    - Twist at the trunk, looking side to side.
  - Beach clean-up: walk around the area bending down to pick up litter.
  - Go for a swim: Perform the breaststroke, backstroke, or front crawl.
  - Yippee, it's summer: Cartwheel around the area.
  - Fun in the sand: Crab-walk to the other side of the playing area.
  - Fishing:
    - Lean back and cast off by tossing a fishing line out into the water.
    - Roll arms to reel the fish in.
- Students form a circle in the gym or playing area.

How to Play

1. One student runs in, retrieves a fitness card from the recycling bin, and performs the fitness activity for 10 to 15 seconds or 10 to 15 reps, depending on the activity.
2. The class follows the student leader by performing the same fitness activity.
3. All students take turns choosing a fitness activity and leading it.

Variations

- Students select a different method of locomotion each time to retrieve a fitness activity (e.g., walk in, skip in, run in, crab-walk in).
- Divide students into four groups and place them in the corners of the gym or playing area:
  - One student runs in, retrieves a fitness activity, and returns to the group.
  - The whole group performs the fitness activity together.
  - All group members have a chance to retrieve a fitness activity.
- Challenge students to create new fitness activities.
- Use fitness activity cards cut into seasonal shapes (e.g., leaf, flower, snowflake).

Eco Thought

This fall, take time to enjoy the autumn colors. Go for a walk, jump in a pile of leaves, visit a national park or conservation area, or rustle up a neighborhood game of football!

Equipment

- A minimum of 10 pieces of recycled paper with fitness activities written on them
- 1 recycling bin

Setup

- Place the physical fitness cards in the recycling bin in the middle of the gym or playing area.
  - Rake the leaves: Extend your arms out and to the side and pull back in a raking motion, then switch sides.
  - Roll the garden hose: Pull in the hose by rolling arms continuously in a circle.
  - Put away the summer toys:
    - Run to the four corners of the gym or playing area.
    - Pretend to pick up a toy in each corner (you may use beanbags).
    - Bring it back to the center of the playing area.
  - Weed the garden: Kneel on one knee and pull up the weeds in front and to the sides; switch arms and knees.
  - Trim the trees: Reach arms overhead, then lower arms to the side, and then cross them overhead.
  - Pick up litter in the yard: Forward lunge across the area to pick up litter.
  - Fertilize the lawn: Pivot on the spot, underhand tossing the fertilizer and alternating hands.
  - Water the lawn:
    - Place one hand on hip, the other hand out to the side.
    - Move hand in a jerking motion across the body (to illustrate the movement of a sprinkler) and sweep arm back to starting point.
    - Switch hands.
- Students form a circle in the gym or playing area.

How to Play

1. One student runs in, retrieves a fitness card from the recycling bin, and performs the fitness activity for 10 to 15 seconds or 10 to 15 reps, depending on the activity.
2. The class follows the student leader by performing the same fitness activity.
3. All students take turns choosing a fitness activity and leading it.

Variations

- Students select a different method of locomotion each time to retrieve a fitness activity (e.g., walk in, skip in, run in, crab-walk in).
- Divide students into four groups and place them in the corners of the gym or playing area.
  - One student runs in, retrieves a fitness activity, and returns to the group.
  - The whole group performs the fitness task together.
  - All group members have a chance to retrieve a fitness activity.
- Challenge students to create new fitness activities.
- Use fitness activity cards cut into seasonal shapes (e.g., leaf, flower, snowflake).

COOPERATIVE ACTIVITIES

When you plant a tree, never plant only one. Plant three—
one for shade, one for fruit, one for beauty.

—African proverb

Cooperative games are positive, motivating, and fun. They promote teamwork, creative thinking, and problem solving. Each game challenges students in activities in which everyone can participate and achieve success. We all win when we take responsibility for greening our world.

BIN BALL RECYCLING

Eco Thought

Using recyclable items as equipment offers a new spin on traditional games. Challenge your friends to come up with a new game using recyclable materials and play it together.

Equipment

- 1 piece of recycled paper crumpled into a ball per team
- 1 recycling bin per team

Setup

- Divide the class into two teams with players scattered throughout the classroom.
- Place a recycling bin at both the front and back of the playing area.
- Players remain at their desks or at a designated spot in the playing area.

How to Play

1. Players pass a crumpled-paper ball around the classroom until it gets to a teammate who is close enough to score a basket in the recycling bin.
2. Players must pass the paper ball a minimum of three times to three different players before attempting to score.
3. Players score two points per basket.
4. Players may pass and shoot to score and may block the other team's passes and shots.
5. Play until time is called by the teacher.

Note

Designate one player per team to retrieve missed shots.

Variations

- To increase the challenge of the game, add two or three paper balls per team.
- After playing for two or three minutes, all players switch places and continue playing.
- Play until you reach a set score.

Adapted, by permission, from Peel District School Board, 2006, *Hooked on DPA-Daily physical activity* (Mississauga, ON: Peel District School Board).

LITTER NOT!

Eco Thought

Imagine what the world would be like if everyone littered and no one picked up garbage? Litter attracts bugs and rats that spread diseases. Reducing litter helps improve the quality of life for humans, animals, and the natural environment. Litter not!

Equipment

- 1 recycling bin
- 50 to 100 balls (or beanbags or a combination)

Setup

- Scatter the balls around the playing area.
- Place a large recycling bin in the center of the playing area.

How to Play

1. Players scatter around the playing area and wait for the signal to begin.
2. On the go signal, players pick up litter by retrieving the balls. Players may pick up just one ball at a time.
3. Players return the ball to the recycling bin.
4. Once all of the balls are in the recycling bin, the game begins again.

Variations

- The teacher or a player tosses the balls back into the playing area for continuous play.

- Players perform a ball skill, such as tossing it to themselves and catching it or bouncing the ball, before placing it in the bin.
- Designate a line on the ground as the shooting line; players stand at the line and shoot the ball into the bin.

KNOCK OUT POLLUTION

Eco Thought

If we take a closer look, a lot of our garbage is really made up of reusable and recyclable materials. How much of it could you reuse or recycle instead of throwing it away? Help knock out pollution!

Equipment

- At least 30 plastic soda bottles of various sizes
- Soft balls, sock balls, or beanbags (2 per student)

Setup

- Place the plastic bottles equally spaced along the centerline of the gym or playing area.
- Divide the class into two teams.
- Set up a safety zone for each team approximately 10 feet (3 m) from the plastic bottles.
- Players must throw the ball from behind the safety zone line.

How to Play

1. Provide each team with several balls of various sizes.
2. On the go signal, players throw underhand to knock down the plastic bottles.
3. The activity is restarted when all of the pins are knocked down or when time is called.

Note

Players may use an overhand throw or soccer kick, to knock down the plastic bottles.

Variations

- Once the initial game is played, challenge players by providing a point system for each type of bottle (e.g., small = 5 points, large = 2 points, colored = 3 points, clear = 1 point).

- Players may track their own score.
- Challenge players to create another game using the plastic bottles and share it with the class.

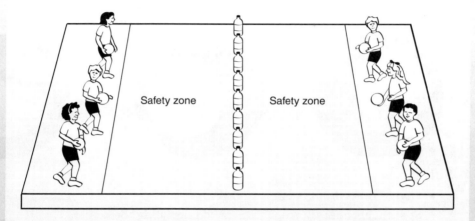

Eco Thought

When we practice the three Rs, we buy less stuff and help minimize the amount of greenhouse gases we add to the earth's atmosphere. When shopping, ask yourself whether you really need something before buying it, take a reusable bag, and try to buy things that are made from recycled materials.

Equipment

- 3 recyclable items (e.g., water bottles, plastic containers) or beanbags per team
- 1 recycling bin or plastic hoop

Setup

- Divide the class into teams of three.
- Space teams evenly around a large circle facing the center.
- Players in each team of three sit one behind the other.
- Assign each player a name: Reduce, Reuse, or Recycle.
- Place several recyclable items inside a recycling bin in the middle of the circle.

How to Play

1. Teacher calls out one of the three names (e.g., Reduce).
   - All the players named Reduce jump up and run around the outside of the circle and around the teams in a clockwise direction.
   - Reuse and Recycle form an arch waiting for their teammate to return.
   - Upon returning, Reduce runs under the arch toward the middle, takes a recyclable item, and holds it high in the air.
   - Players try to reach the center of the circle first.
2. Once completed, the players return the recyclable items to the bin in the middle of the circle and listen for the next name to be called.
3. Play continues until all players have had a turn.

Notes

- Players can only run when their name is called.
- Be sure the recyclable items are safe and clean.

Variations

- Include one less beanbag than the number of teams.
- Change the names to represent other green themes (e.g., Oak, Maple, Pine or Bottle, Can, Paper).

GREEN-TEAM CATCH

Eco Thought

When it comes to helping the environment, it's the little things that count. Switching off the lights, turning off the taps, and using both sides of paper all adds up. Set an example, and your ideas will catch on!

Equipment

- A variety of soft balls (5 to 8 per team)
- 4 pylons or lines in the gym

Setup

- Divide the class into two teams.
- Each team chooses a player to be the environmental catcher.
- The environmental catcher crosses over to the opposite side and stands on a line at the back of the other team's zone.
- Create a safe zone around the environmental catchers to protect them from collisions with opposing players.
- Opposing players try to catch, intercept, or block balls from reaching the environmental catcher.

How to Play

1. Players stay on their side of the playing area and throw a ball toward the environmental catcher.
2. If the environmental catcher catches the ball cleanly, the thrower becomes an environmental catcher and joins his or her teammate on the line.
3. If an environmental catcher falls off the line while attempting to catch a ball, he or she must return to his or her team's side to continue throwing balls to a catcher.
4. The game is over when one team has all of its players on the line.

Variations

- Team members stand on a mat or a bench, depending on age and grade level. If players fall off the mat or bench, they must return to their team's side to continue throwing balls to a catcher.
- If the original environmental catcher falls off the line while trying to catch a ball, the game is over. Choose a new environmental catcher and start again.

Adapted, by permission, from CIRA, 1998, Bench ball. In *Great gator games* (Ontario, Canada: Canadian Intramural Recreation Association of Ontario), 7.

READY, SET, COMPOST

Eco Thought

Don't throw away those veggie peels! Use them to create your own compost. Composting lets you turn leaves, food scraps, and even paper into rich brown soil that is great for your garden and saves space in our landfills.

Equipment

- A minimum of 75 colored beanbags:
  - Brown = soil
  - Yellow = air
  - Red = vegetable and fruit peels
  - Green = leaves, grass clippings
  - Blue = water
- 4 plastic hoops

Setup

- Divide players into four groups.
- Place each team into a corner of the playing area.
- Place one plastic hoop in each corner to represent the team's composter.
- Place a pile of compost material (beanbags) into the middle of the playing area.
- Line up each team behind or around its composter.

How to Play

1. On the go signal, all players run to the center of the playing area to retrieve one item for composting and race back to place it in their composter. Each team needs to collect beanbags of every color.
2. Continue until all compost material is gone from the middle of the playing area.
3. At this point, players may begin to steal one compost item at a time from any of the other teams' composters.
4. After two to three minutes, the teacher says, "Compost!" and all players stop immediately and return to their team's composter to count the items.
5. Acknowledge the number of items each team has collected and congratulate them for composting!
6. Return all beanbags to the middle of the gym and play again.

Notes

- Players may take only one beanbag at a time.
- Players may not prevent others from taking items from their composter.
- Beanbags must be placed in the composter, not thrown.

KEEP ON RECYCLIN'

Eco Thought

The choices we make every day have an impact on the environment. When we throw stuff away it usually ends up in a landfill, a giant garbage dump where we bury trash. Recycling helps reduce trash. Keep on recycling!

Equipment

- 10 pieces of recycled paper per 2 students
- 1 plastic lid per student (or cardboard box lids or clipboards)
- 4 to 8 recycling bins (or cardboard boxes or buckets)

Setup

- Divide the class into pairs.
- Spread the pairs along the sidelines on either side of the gym or playing area.
- Place several recycling bins along the centerline of the playing area.
- Give each pair a stack of recycled paper and one lid per player.

How to Play

1. On the go signal, one partner crumples a piece of paper into a ball.
2. Players use their plastic lids to hit the paper ball back and forth to each other, trying not to let it drop, while at the same time moving toward the recycling bin.
3. Once partners reach the recycling bin, they use their lids to hit their paper ball into the bin for a point.
4. Pairs run back to their starting line, crumple another piece of paper, and begin again.

Notes

- If the paper ball drops while moving toward the bin, players stop, pick it up, and continue.

- Missed shots are left on the floor and no points are awarded.
- Lids of any size will work; however, the larger the lid, the easier it is for students to play.

RECYCLING-BIN BASKETBALL

Eco Thought

Get involved and start a home recycling center. Teach your family the basics of recycling by showing them how to separate plastic, paper, cardboard, and glass. Use your blue bin for a greener future!

Equipment

- 2 recycling bins per team
- 1 soft ball per team
- 1 pinny or vest per student
- 2 plastic hoops per team

Setup

- Divide the class into four teams (two teams per court).
- Each team chooses one teammate to stand in the basketball key area or in a plastic hoop as the recycling-bin catcher.
- The recycling-bin catcher holds a recycling bin or bucket.
- Use pylons to mark the key area five steps away from the hoop.

How to Play

1. The game is played as a typical basketball game with the following modifications:
   - Players score in their own recycling bin.
   - The recycling-bin catcher may assist teammates by moving the bin to help them score a point.
   - Players may only pass the ball, no dribbling.
   - Players must pass the ball a minimum of three times to three different players before attempting to score.
   - Players score two points per basket.
2. After a recycling-bin basket is scored, the defending team clears the zone.
3. A player from the opposing team removes the ball from the recycling bin and passes it to a teammate to resume play.

Notes

- One point is deducted if the recycling-bin catcher steps out of the hoop or out of the key area.
- Change the recycling-bin catcher frequently.

50 WAYS TO PITCH IN AND DO YOUR PART

Our hope is to inspire others to make a difference by showing how every little bit counts when it comes to caring for and respecting the earth. Together with our students we have generated the following eco tips. We encourage you to try some of these environmentally friendly ideas with your students and create some of your own to add to the list.

HOME

Encourage responsible environmental practices at home:

- Reduce the amount of electricity you use at home:
  - Turn off the lights when you leave the room.
  - Turn off computer monitors when not in use.
  - Use cold water when you do the laundry.
  - Use a power bar and turn off all of your electronic devices when you are not using them or are not home.
  - Run the dishwasher only when it's full.
  - Turn your air conditioning up a few degrees.
  - Use a fan instead of air conditioning.
  - Turn the heat down and put on a sweater.
  - Change to low-energy lightbulbs.
  - Clean or replace your furnace filter regularly.
- Use electronic methods such as e-mail and websites instead of printing and photocopying.
- Declare a waste-free day.
- Use reusable mugs, plates, and cutlery.
- Use both sides of the paper before recycling.

- Turn off the television and participate in a family activity:
  - Go for a walk.
  - Play at the park.
  - Enjoy a family hike.
  - Observe nature.
  - Go for a bike ride.
  - Get outside and be active with your family.
- Take reusable bags for grocery shopping.
- Buy products that use less packaging.
- Turn off the tap when brushing your teeth.
- Recycle old electronics.
- Help our natural environment:
  - Leave grass clippings on the lawn.
  - Make a bird or animal feed station.
  - Plant a flower or vegetable garden.
  - Plant a tree.
  - Compost garden waste.
- Open the windows and let the fresh air in.
- Set up a recycling area in your home for newsprint, glass, cans, cardboard, and plastic.
- Support local farmers and buy your fruit and vegetables close to home.
- Visit a local conservation area or national park.
- Participate in Earth Hour: For one hour turn everything off.

SCHOOL

Inspire students to understand, appreciate, and take action toward environmental issues:

- Highlight environmental education by celebrating Earth Month, Earth Week, and Earth Day, April 22.
- Participate in Earth Hour: For one hour turn everything off.
- Host an environmentally friendly play day.
- Start an environmental club or committee:
  - Hold an event each month to bring awareness to the issues.

- o Invite guest speakers, such as environmentalists and wildlife presenters.
- o Write a letter or start a petition to your local politicians about an environmental issue or concern.
- Attend workshops and conferences on environmental issues.
- Be a role model.
- Share eco facts during the school announcements or in the school's monthly newsletter.
- Go for a community walk and enjoy the natural environment.
- Challenge local grocery stores to use less packaging.
- Create an eco tree where students attach a written pledge for the environment.
- Host an environmental festival.
- Clean up the community.
- Start a recycling club.
- Host a science fair on an environmental theme.
- Start a walk-to-school program.
- Encourage your school community to leave their cars at home: Walk, bike, or blade to school.
- Adopt a neighborhood pond or stream; learn about it and keep it clean.
- Invent your own recycling game and play it with your students.
- Move outside:
  - o Teach your lessons outdoors.
  - o Create an outdoor classroom.
  - o Start a school garden.
- Green your lunches:
  - o Bring reusable containers for lunch, snacks, and staff meetings.
  - o Host a waste-free lunch day challenge.
  - o Promote litterless lunch kits and recyclable water bottles.
- Create a musical or dance routine using recyclable materials.
- Use both sides of the paper before recycling.
- Collect dead batteries and ink cartridges for recycling.
- Create art posters and sculptures using recyclable materials.

COMMUNITY

Show your support for local environmental events in your community:

- Volunteer at community events.
  - Participate in a community cleanup.
  - Organize a Pick Up Litter Day.
  - Organize a Clean Up the Beach Day, Park Day, and so on.
  - Participate in a local tree planting initiative.
- Host a neighborhood yard sale: One person's trash is another person's treasure.
- Encourage your community to leave their cars at home: Walk, bike, or blade to school, work, and the grocery store.
- Collect or donate items for your local reuse center.
- Use reusable containers for lunch or snacks.
- Take a recyclable water bottle or coffee mug to meetings or events.
- Encourage local stores to provide recycling depots for dead batteries, ink cartridges, and electronics.
- Donate unwanted clothing to a local charity.
- Hold a book exchange with friends or coworkers.
- Share eco facts in your community newsletter, local newspaper, and elsewhere.

RECOMMENDED RESOURCES

David Suzuki Foundation: Solutions Are in Our Nature—www.davidsuzuki.org

Earth Day Canada—www.earthday.ca

Keep America Beautiful: Litter Prevention, Waste Reduction, Beautification—www.kab.org

National Geographic Kids: Kids' Games, Animals, Photos, Stories, and More—www.kids.nationalgeographic.com

Nature Conservancy: Protecting Nature, Preserving Life—www.nature.org

United Nations Environment Programme: TUNZA Children and Youth—www.unep.org/tunza

World Wildlife Federation—www.wwf.panda.org

ABOUT THE AUTHORS

Carol Scaini, MEd, is a health and physical education teacher, guidance counselor, and member of the environmental team at Treeline Public School in Brampton, Ontario, Canada. Scaini is also a part-time health and physical education additional qualification instructor at the Ontario Institute for Studies in Education/University of Toronto (OISE/UT) and a part-time instructor in the department of education at Tyndale University College in Toronto.

An experienced educator, Scaini is a frequent presenter at health and physical education conferences and has authored several health and physical education resources for a number of nonprofit organizations and health and physical education organizations.

Scaini is a member of Physical and Health Education Canada's Health Promoting Schools Program Advisory Committee (HPS PAC) and an executive member of the Ontario Association for the Supervision of Physical Education and Health Education (OASPHE).

In 2011, Scaini earned an Award of Distinction from the Peel District School Board. She received the Dr. Andy Anderson Young Professional Award from PHE Canada in 2007 and the Prime Minister's Award for Teaching Excellence in 2001. That same year, Scaini received the honor of Ontario Teacher of the Year.

In her free time, Scaini enjoys exercise, photography, technology, and time with her nieces, nephews, family, and friends. She resides in Toronto, Ontario.

Carolyn Evans, BEdu, is a teacher librarian with the Peel District in Mississauga, Ontario. She is also the coordinator of school environmental initiatives and chairperson of the school green team. With a passion for health and environmental issues in education, Carolyn has 30 years of teaching experience in physical education, classroom, special education, and library.

Evans has been a workshop presenter at various school, board, and provincial conferences and has developed various resources in health and physical education for not-for-profit and health and physical education organizations.

In 2007, Evans was given an Award of Distinction from the Peel Board of Education for her exemplary work on the Daily Physical Activity Implementation Committee. In 2010, she was nominated for the Prime Minister's Award, a national award in recognition of teaching excellence' the Premier's Award, a provincial award for excellence in leadership; and another Award of Distinction from the Peel Board of Education.

Evans is a member of Physical and Health Education Canada (PHE Canada), Ontario Physical Health and Education Association (OPHEA), Canadian Intramural and Recreation Association (CIRA), HPE steering committees with Peel District School Board, ECOKIDS. ca, and Schools for a Living Planet–World Wildlife Federation (WWF).

In her free time, Evans enjoys being active with her family in the great outdoors, gardening, and reading.

You'll find other outstanding games resources at
www.HumanKinetics.com

In the U.S. call 1.800.747.4457
Australia 08 8372 0999
Canada 1.800.465.7301
Europe . . . . .+44 (0) 113 255 5665
New Zealand . . . 0064 9 448 1207

HUMAN KINETICS
The Information Leader in Physical Activity
P.O. Box 5076 • Champaign, IL 61825-5076